RENOIR

A GIRL WITH A WATERING CAN   1876   Oil   39½" x 28¾"
National Gallery of Art, Washington, D. C. Chester Dale Collection (Loan)

PIERRE AUGUSTE
RENOIR

by

ROSAMUND FROST

Published by
THE HYPERION PRESS
NEW YORK

THIS VOLUME,

ONE OF THE HYPERION ART MONOGRAPHS,

WAS EDITED BY AIMÈE CRANE

AND PUBLISHED IN MCMXLIV FOR

THE HYPERION PRESS

Printed in the United States of America

Copyright 1944, by The Hyperion Press, New York

RENOIR

Our Foremost Modern Old Master
Re-estimated a Quarter Century After His Death

by ROSAMUND FROST

Why another book on Renoir?

Because he painted nearly 5,000 pictures, more than any other single important modern artist. Because he represents the creative stream that opposed and paralleled Cubism and its outgrowths — a movement which today, after several decades underground, is due for a rebirth, if only out of reaction. Above all Renoir is our foremost modern old master. We accept his pictures, as we accept the great compositions of Titian and Poussin and Delacroix, without demanding of them references to the times we live in. A quarter century after his death, in the violence and tension of this particular moment in world history, Renoir gains stature through the utter detachment and deliberation of his statement. For, as he himself observed, "The simplest subjects are eternal."

If Renoir is classic, his is no case of a man born fifty years too late. His work bridges right into our time and, unlike the other Impressionists, only a minor portion of it is historic. But it is traditional in the broadest sense. Past the turn into the modern age, even through the First World War, he went on quietly expanding the lessons learned of Courbet and Delacroix, of the eighteenth century, and of the Venetians. It can be safely said that the grand tradition of figure painting survived actively in Renoir's person until December 1919 and that through his followers countless echoes of it are still rolling around today.

The appreciation of Renoir down the years makes a fascinating record of changing thought. Vollard was the first to remark how his career had something magic about it. For, the contemporary prejudice against Impressionism once overcome, it never suffered a setback or even the usual period of outgrowth by which the world likes to test the ultimate staying powers of its favorites. Succeeding generations have sought and found in him what they needed. In the 1880s Renoir's growing list of portrait commissions were doubtless largely due to the wonderfully bad taste of the milieu he describes so accurately — the Turkey carpets, the pedestalled palms, the fretted screens which contribute to the sumptuous stuffiness

COUNTRY DANCE
c. 1890   Soft ground etching   8 9/16" x 5 9/16"
Courtesy of The Art Institute of Chicago, The Albert Roullier Memorial Collection

of the upper bourgeois interior. The likenesses of his early patroness Mme. Charpentier, of Mme. Caillebotte, and the rest of them hold a corresponding "charm" for us — which they obviously didn't for the sitters, who probably saw themselves as the embodiment of sophisticated elegance. But one thing is sure: to each of them Renoir is able to give an extraordinary glow and sense of life.

The strange thing is how the exquisite subtleties of Renoir's painting passed virtually unnoticed in his own time. Instead, criticism dwelt on its coarseness and lack of finish. Even super-cerebrals like the Goncourts, who re-introduced their contemporaries to the eighteenth century, were too close to the artist to see in him the successor of the Watteau and Fragonard they admired.

Renoir's early champions were soon justified. His Durand-Ruel retrospective of 1883 was a semi-success. By the 1890s the pecuniary struggle was over, even though an incorrigible naturalness continued to bewilder such genuinely admiring critics as Arsène Alexandre, who in 1892 refers to ". . . the treasures of a gifted child." But by 1907 the straight painting quality of his early work began to be apparent to almost everybody, and the portrait of Mme. Charpentier, once commissioned for 300 francs, sold for 84,000. In another ten years the advance-guard, for whom Fauvism and Expressionism had lifted the ban on "unnatural" color and form, were beginning to sense the powerful monumentality of his red-suffused late period. By 1919 Renoir had lived to be decorated by the French Government and to revisit his own pictures in the Louvre.

In our day we can view Renoir down the small end of the telescope. If the sculptor Bourdelle was the first to make the tie-up with the classic pattern, countless books have since been written echoing with comparisons to the great names of the past, laden with pastry-rich words to describe the overflowing bounty of his work. So it is primarily as a master figure painter that Renoir takes his place in our scheme of things. At the same time we can enjoy his passionate naturalism, his shimmering touch, his unique tenderness in the literally hundreds of smaller canvases which the unparalleled vogue for Renoir has brought to America.

Renoir's life was such a quiet one that even small events raised a ripple which eventually carried to his whole work. The magnetic pole of his career is the Sèvres factory at Limoges, in which provincial center he was born in 1841. Though the family moved to Paris soon after and it was in the capital that the boy first became an apprentice at the fine art of decorating china with a brush, no doubt but that local pride in the home town's most respected industry directed the application of his early talent for drawing.

In later years Renoir was to observe to Vollard that he had always permitted life to carry him in its current rather than make his own decisions. This is borne out by the next step in his career. It was the invention of the decalcomania, together with the new cult for machine-decorated objects (which was soon to find its expression in the Exposition Universelle of 1867) that brought to a close what might otherwise have been a life's occupation. In the workshop of a maker of hand-painted awnings, signs, and backdrops, Renoir was soon able to expand the conventional medallions and orderly flowerets through which, since the age of thirteen, he had been learning to steady his hand and tune his eye to the innocent pinks, blues and greens, to the radiant porcelain whites that we encounter over and again in his early easel painting.

Two other developments stemmed from this job. The first originated in the demand for decorations in the eighteenth century style, which necessitated familiarity with the models for their mincing coquetries — the great Bouchers and Fragonards of the Louvre, onto whose tradition Renoir's work inextricably links. The second was the fact that it paid good enough money to enable him at the age of nineteen to take off a whole year and study painting in the studio of the academician Gleyre. Though until 1865 part-time practical jobs were needed to eke out, Renoir from this day forward could give his entire heart and mind to expressing himself with a brush.

"I presume you are painting to amuse yourself," was the first remark that Gleyre addressed to the new pupil, the tailor's

BABY   c. 1902   Pastel drawing   24½" x 18½"
The Buffalo Fine Arts Academy, Albright Art Gallery

6

ODALISQUE 1870 Oil 27" x 48½"
National Gallery of Art, Washington, D. C. Chester Dale Collection (Loan)

BATHERS WITH A CRAB   1892 Oil 21½" x 26¼"
Durand-Ruel

YOUNG GIRL LOOKING AT THE FLOWERS
1916 Oil 12¾" x 12¼"
Farnsworth Museum, Wellesley College

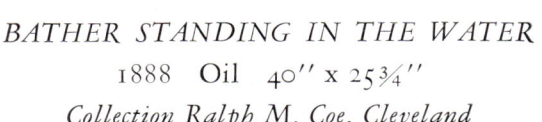

YOUNG SHEPHERD WITH BIRDS
1911   Oil   29½" x 36½"
Durand-Ruel

BATHER STANDING IN THE WATER
1888   Oil   40" x 25¾"
Collection Ralph M. Coe, Cleveland

PEACHES Oil *Private Collection*

JUDGMENT OF PARIS   1908-10   Sanguine drawing   18½" x 23¾"
The Phillips Memorial Gallery, Washington, D. C.

son who had earned his living at commercial art. "I most certainly am," answered Renoir. From the start his pleasure in his profession is so obvious that it awakens a corresponding enjoyment in us today. Even in the early near-genre pictures done in the Forest of Fontainebleau under the stimulation of his companionship with Manet, Sisley, and Bazille (co-pupils at the Gleyre academy) there is a rare sense of satisfaction and fulfillment. The Manet influence was present too, for Manet, older, worldly, the bearer of what passed as dangerous artistic gifts, was the proper idol of a younger painter. He lorded it over the Café Guerbois group which Renoir timidly began to frequent — a group which included such literary and artistic figures as only nineteenth century Paris could have assembled under one roof. Yet, while Renoir adopted many of Manet's brush simplifications, the blacks which began to appear in his pictures never had that harsh almost Spanish elegance. They were merely foils for pale pearly tones common to all the Impressionists but used in Renoir's case with more love for the subjects than scientific interest in the properties of light.

About 1868 Renoir began frequenting the *grenouillères* (literally translated "frog-holes") of the Seine — those amicable little waterfront restaurants at Asnières and Argenteuil, at Bougival and Marly where the rustling city folk played at being rustic. Manet the dandy had made them fashionable with the artistic set. Courbet had proved how paintable they were. It took Renoir to turn them into lusty poetry. First he described the locale, in relatively thick color as an Impressionist might: the glint of water, the rustle of trees, the bridges and landings, terraces and tables. Later the amateur oarsmen themselves appear and the girls who step so diffidently yet gracefully into their boats. Their conversational exchanges have the liveliness of Offenbach music, tunes which frequently accompanied such river outings. There is a "party" feeling to it all which makes a festive parallel to Renoir's more personalized portraits, to his purely painterly experiments, and to what was soon to become for him the great, the eternal subject: the female nude.

The War of 1870 made no perceptible break in Renoir's work and it is consoling for us today to reflect how little mark

11

a German occupation left on Paris itself. Renoir's *Pont Neuf* of 1872 is perhaps the most becoming portrait ever painted of this queen of cities. We are shown it of an early morning, quivering with air, glistening with light even in the shadows — those living blue shadows which he reserved for Paris scenes and which became such a source of ridicule in the second Impressionist show of 1877, his second appearance with the group. On this occasion he presented a view of an open-air dancehall aflicker with golden lights — an incomparably gay picture which conveys the whole story of his Montmartre days. Its subjects were the volatile, easy-living Paris midinettes whom we recognize by their engaging ways and their little cat faces in the majority of the paintings between 1875 and 1883. Some were the mistresses of his friends, others girls whose looks he had fancied and whom he bribed to pose for him by offerings of hats. Renoir never tired of trying hats on women and his barest studio was usually brightened by bonnets of all descriptions. It was this atmosphere and these models that introduce the note of pleasure and informality in the work of 1879 and the early '80s — a far cry from the tight-buttoned formality of Seurat, the cynical demi-monde of Lautrec, or Degas' strained, nervous world of backstage.

As much as any nineteenth century psychological novelist, Renoir is the master of personal relationships. As an undercurrent to all his work there runs an eloquent dialogue of human feelings, betrayed in the casual glance, the accidental gesture, or the transient expression. We sense the persuasiveness of one character, the confidence of another. He shows us intimate exchanges over the breakfast table, the shared enjoyment of a young couple reading, the eager collaboration of two girls at the piano, tender relationships with children. Long after the necessity for executing group portrait commissions had passed, it amused him to exercise his skill in laying open this interweaving of human lives. By 1881 these elements are joined to the attributes of great figure composition. The spectator gets the feeling of the infinite riches of the physical world spread forth on a perfect summer afternoon. There is greater depth, more complex grouping, a new warmth of palette which raises the colors of air and water, of flesh and fruits and stuffs to a single high-pitched vibration — the key in which Renoir was increasingly to paint.

In 1879 Renoir took a brief trip to Algeria, thereby satisfying a common weakness of the time: the taste for the exotic which had received its impetus from Napoleon's Egyptian campaign, had reached its heights in the paintings of Delacroix, and was to unburden itself in a flood of late nineteenth century novels. Already back in 1870 he had unleashed his imaginings on a lavishly bedizened odalisque. In '72 he composed a canvas after Delacroix's *Women of Algiers*, a harem scene of patently fancy-dress order. If such subject matter only occasionally recurred in his painting, it was to serve every time as a proving ground for a new and wider palette, with more hot tones and more unexpected juxtaposition of color.

SEATED WOMAN   Pencil drawing   14 3/16" x 11 5/16"
The Art Institute of Chicago, Samuel P. Avery Fund Collection

His next trip, to Italy in 1881, took effect slowly but is commonly cited as the cause for the well-known break in the middle of his work — the gradual tightening of forms and retreat into a dry, almost fresco palette — which began about 1883 and reached its heights in paintings like *Battledore and Shuttlecock*, which in turn plays on the formal rhythms of the eighteenth century. It was Renoir's answer to the critics who accused him of being unable to draw, perhaps also an unconscious urge to recapture the solidity of his early style. Many pencil studies and small watercolors date from this period, the latter of a detail and finish worthy of his porcelain-painting days.

By the late 1880s the disciplinary phase was over and with it all dependence on styles and cultures foreign to his own. The Impressionists, Delacroix, the Italian masters sank rapidly over the horizon for an artist whose world, as he grew older, increasingly narrowed down to the few places and faces he loved. Ten years after, even Rome seemed to him a "museum city" of too many churches, too many masterpieces. As the multiple interests of the late century reached outwards, Renoir retreated into the classic example of bourgeois chauvinism, impatient of intellectuals, suspicious of everything "exotic," which for him soon came to mean anything that was not French. Since his marriage he had become more and more of a stranger to the salon world of Mme. Charpentier. The homely wisdom that he craved he now rediscovered in the fables of La Fontaine. Perhaps no other artist has so capitalized on provincialism and at the same time made us so aware of its basic worth and strength.

The Renoir type is probably the most consistent female in all of modern painting. From the piquante little midinette, she flowers into magnificent maturity, her features set for all time by the girl he married in 1881, one Alice Changiat. Virtually every subsequent portrait gives a hint of the pointed smile, of those wide-set kitten eyes and the soft, provocative middle-class face which somehow is not incongruous on the ripe, heavy bodies he admired. Renoir never painted a thin woman or a woman who wore a corset. Riches for him lay in calm, deep-breathing, abundant health, as we find it in the bathers that begin to appear around 1889-90. It has been pointed out that, to judge from the artistic record, the late nineteenth century was a very well scrubbed period, full of women dousing themselves in basins and drying their limbs. Degas' went at it so hard you feel they are taking the skin off. But not so Renoir's. Their serene animalism and utter relaxation, their innocence in a day when Lautrec and Forain had attached an unsavory character to nudity, builds still another link between Renoir and the tradition of Giorgione, Titian, and Poussin.

Characteristically, the next turning point in Renoir's career was the outcome of no personal decision. It was at the urgent insistence of his doctor that the artist first went to the south of France whose climate was so decisively to influence his palette. A severe bronchitis of 1882 had been the first herald of increasingly bad health. 1889 brought further physical setbacks in the form of facial paralysis and a nagging rheumatism which within five years had him completely dependent on a cane. Successive winters saw the Renoir family at numerous small Riviera resorts until, in 1906, he settled once and for all in Cagnes, building his house among the ancient twisted olives which lend their rhythms to so many of his late compositions.

Though it has been claimed that landscape for Renoir was a distraction between figure pieces, in the long run it was mainly through it that he developed his technical and color innovations. As an Impressionist, nature had looked to him blue-green, airy, sun-flecked. From here he worked toward more tufty, cottony textures. After the "dry" period the scene becomes more dappled, more organic, more suited to contain figures. Under the sun of the south it takes on a hot aromatic flavor. The writhing limbs of olive trees serve for experiments along the lines that Delacroix laid down when he advocated modeling trees by twisting masses and giving prime importance to the flesh-colored counter-reflection. Renoir's control over this play of half-tones is one of the most astonishing things about his late work. Figures and landscape become inseparably interwoven. The nude dissolves her color in nature which reflects it back in the form of brilliant light, high, sustained, persistent as the note of cicadas in August. In the late '90s there comes a new mastery in the grouping of figures. He has learned how to bind them together in deep space by means of action that passes from one to the other — something no artist had attempted for over a century.

If landscape became a means to an end, flowers, said Renoir, "rest my brain." Perhaps because he had painted so many decorative ones in his early teens, he makes little pretence toward arranging them. The approach is as varied as it is unpredictable: some are all scent and texture, like the really breath-taking *Lilacs*, others purely arbitrary. They might be made of cotton or velvet or folded paper, not too far removed from the imitation bouquet that to this day ornaments the main table of the French small bourgeois drawing-room. On the whole vegetables and fruits invited him more in their living roundness, whether the subject was a melting sliced canteloupe, bloomy peaches, or some really distractingly lovely pink onions.

When Renoir married he automatically became a family artist. Turning as ever to the subjects nearest at hand, he painted his children and the faithful maids, who at any time were ready to do double duty as models. Mme. Renoir was presumably too busy keeping this invalid-centered household on an even keel to pose often, but he does occasionally show her to us, kindly and competent, shrewd in the French homemaking sense. The artist's special darling was his youngest son, Coco. We meet him in all the beguiling stages between babyhood and boyhood in perhaps the finest series of children's pictures ever painted.

As Renoir's disabilities shut down his world about him the figure composition comes into its own. Flesh becomes moun-

ORANGE SELLER   Sanguine drawing

tainous, canvases are "full to bursting," a kind of saturation of space by form. The technique has changed greatly too, and is to change still further as his paralyzed hands feel increasing pain in holding the brush. After 1900 Renoir strives for thick unctuous surfaces which, as he says, "can carry their varnish," and looks back on his Impressionist brushwork as "something to scratch matches on." His friend Albert André, himself a painter, gives us the best account of how he went about this. After roughly indicating his volumes in red-brown underpaint, Renoir would give the canvas a light wash of color thinned in turpentine. The faint forms that now appear are strengthened with pigment dissolved in pure oil and highlights are indicated. Out of a haze the picture slowly emerges, rather like the magical self-printing of a photographic plate. There are neither extreme highlights nor dark shadows but the colors fuse into one another and lap the limbs into roundness. Rose-red dominates the palette, often overflowing from the figures to invade the air itself. Many people who otherwise admire Renoir find this red dominance unaesthetic, hard to take. It becomes more comprehensible if considered not as a natural color but as one conventional and symbolic — the color of life to a man utterly cut off from it, the way the sun looks through the closed eyelids of the very old.

What Renoir accomplished in the last years of his life is no less than amazing. Emaciated, mummy-like, swathed against the chills that had undone him, he painted indefatigably and the whole household turned around his painting. By means of trestles his wheel-chair could be raised to reach inaccessible corners of the canvas. His palette was laid on his knees, brushes were inserted into the twisted, bandaged hands and once in place were rinsed in turpentine rather than changed, still further contributing to the color fusion. At any time Gabrielle, the cook whose skin "took the light," was ready to pose for one of those monumental bathers. To pictures of the last period a classical calm is added to the ever-present desirability of woman which Renoir joked about when he said "A nude is finished when you want to go to bed with it."

Till the very day of his death Renoir worked in the conviction that he was making constant progress. To the end he strove to realize the great figure composition in landscape. As this has been an aim of painters since the Renaissance's rediscovery of Classical antiquity, the form and spirit of his work is familiar. What is new, what brings him close, is its application to a small, tender, personal world. Or as Renoir himself put it quite simply, "'A naked woman will rise from the salt wave, or from her own bed, she will be called Venus or Nini. No one will ever invent anything better than that.''

BIBLIOGRAPHY

Albert André, *Renoir*. Paris, 1919, G. Crès et Cie.

L'Atelier de Renoir. Paris, 1931. Editions Bernheim-Jeune. Avant-propos de M. Albert André.

Albert C. Barnes and Violette de Mazia, *The Art of Renoir*. New York, 1935, Minton, Balch & Co.

Adolphe Basler, *Renoir*, Paris, 1928, Editions de la Nouvelle Revue Française.

Anthony Bertram, *Auguste Renoir*, London, 1935, Studio Publications, World's Masters Series.

Maurice Bérard, *Renoir à Wargemont*, Paris, 1939, Larose.

George Besson, *Renoir*, Paris, 1932, G. Crès et Cie.

Jacques-Emile Blanche, *Propos de Peintres*, Paris, 1919, Emile-Paul.

Gustave Coquiot, *Renoir*, Paris, 1925, Albin Michel.

Théodore Duret, *Renoir*, Paris, 1924, Editions Bernheim-Jeune.

Théodore Duret, *Renoir*, New York, 1937, Crown Publishers. Translated from the French by Madeleine Boyd.

Théodore Duret, *Histoire des Peintres Impressionistes*. Paris, 1906, H. Floury.

Georges Duthuit, *Renoir, Les Contemporains*, Paris, 1923, Stock.

Michel Florisoone, *Renoir*, Paris, 1938, The Hyperion Press.

François Fosca, *Renoir*, New York, 1924, Dodd, Mead and Co. Translated by Hubert Wellington.

Julius Meier-Graefe, *Renoir, Mit Hundert Abbildungen*. München, 1911, R. Piper & Co.

Julius Meier-Graefe, *Renoir*, Paris, 1912, H. Floury. Translated from the German to French by A. S. Maillet.

Julius Meier-Graefe, *Renoir*, Leipzig, 1929, Klinkhardt und Biermann.

The Metropolitan Museum of Art, *Renoir, A Special Exhibition of His Paintings*, May 18-Sept. 12, 1937, New York, 1937, William Bradford Press. Introduction by Harry B. Wehle.

Octave Mirbeau, *Renoir*, Paris, 1913, Bernheim-Jeune.

J. Pascal, *Notices sur Renoir*, Paris, 1904, Societé Parisiennes d'Editeurs.

Renoir, Munich, no date, R. Piper & Co. (Marées Society, Munich).

Renoir, Vingt-huit Reproductions, Paris, 1928, Gallimard. Etude Critique par Adolphe Basler.

Georges Rivière, *Renoir et Ses Amis*, Paris, 1921, H. Floury.

Claude Roger-Marx, *Renoir*, Paris, 1933, H. Floury.

Louis Rousselet, *Notes sur Renoir*, Paris, 1900.

Leo Stein, *Renoir*, Paris, 1928 (?), Librairie de France.

Ten Water Colors, Sanguines and Pastels by Renoir. Geneva, 1921, Editions Georg. Introduction by René Jean. Translated by Ronald Davis.

Jens Peter Thüs, *Kunst, Gammel, Og Ny*. Oslo, 1937, Gyldendal Norsk Forlag.

Ambroise Vollard, *Renoir, An Intimate Record*, New York, 1930, Knopf.

Ambroise Vollard, *La Vie at l'Oeuvre de Pierre Auguste Renoir*, Paris, 1919, Chez Ambroise Vollard.

WARGEMONT ROSES Oil Private Collection

YOUNG GIRLS PLAYING BATTLEDORE AND SHUTTLECOCK   1888   Oil   26″ x 21½″
Collection of The Minneapolis Institute of Arts

AT THE MILLINER'S c. 1876 Oil 12¾" x 9⅝"
The Fogg Museum of Art, Harvard University, Bequest of Annie S. Coburn

MOTHER AND CHILD Oil 39⅜" x 31½"
Albright Art Gallery, Buffalo

NUDE 1892 Oil 25⅜" x 32"
Courtesy of Mr. and Mrs. George Gard De Sylva, Los Angeles

SELF-PORTRAIT c. 1876 Oil 29" x 22½"

Courtesy of Mr. William H. Taylor, Philadelphia

ALFRED SISLEY Oil 25⅝" x 21¼"
The Art Institute of Chicago, Mr. and Mrs. L. L. Coburn Memorial

MONSIEUR CHOQUET   1874   Oil   18" x 14¼"
The Fogg Museum of Art, Harvard University, Winthrop Collection

NUDE SEATED c. 1885 Oil 25″ x 30½″
Musée Rodin, Paris

AFTER THE BATH   1890 Oil 16¾" x 12½"
Collection of Mr. Herman Shulman, Stamford, Conn.

PORTRAIT OF MADAME EDOUARD MAITRE c. 1871 Oil 14¾″ x 12¾″
Collection of the Smith College Museum of Art

LE BAL A BOUGIVAL 1883 Oil 70⅝" x 37¾"
Collection of the Museum of Fine Arts, Boston

REFLECTIONS 1878 Oil 25½" x 21¼"
Courtesy of Dr. Jakob Goldschmidt, New York

LITTLE NUDE IN BLUE c. 1880 Oil 18¼" x 15"
The Buffalo Fine Arts Academy, Albright Art Gallery

WOMAN WRITING 1890 Oil 16" x 12"
Courtesy of Mr. Carroll Carstairs, New York

BOATERS AT BOUGIVAL Oil 21¼" x 25⅝"

Private Collection, San Francisco

SEATED BATHER 1914 Oil 32" x 25½"
Courtesy of Durand-Ruel, New York

THE SEINE AT CHATOU   c. 1871 Oil 18" x 24"
Collection of The Art Gallery of Toronto

CLAUDE AT THE EASEL   c. 1906 Oil
Courtesy of The Metropolitan Museum of Art, New York

MOTHER AND CHILD   Oil   25⅜" x 21"
Private Collection, San Francisco

YOUNG GIRLS AT THE PIANO c. 1883 Oil 21½" x 17½"
Collection of The Society of Liberal Arts, Joslyn Memorial, Omaha

MADAME TILLA DURIEUX 1914 Oil 36½" x 29"
Courtesy of Mr. Stephen C. Clark, New York

BOATING PARTY AT CHATOU　　　　　　　　　　　　　　　　1879 Oil 31⅞" x 39¼"
Courtesy of The Lewisohn Collection, New York

THE ALGERIAN GIRL   1881   Oil   20" x 15¾"
Museum of Fine Arts, Boston

FLOWERS AND PRICKLY PEARS c. 1884 Oil 29" x 23⅜"
Mr. and Mrs. W. W. Crocker Collection, Burlingame, California

IN THE MEADOW c. 1894-5 Oil 32" x 25¾"
Courtesy of The Lewisohn Collection, New York

LE MOULIN DE LA GALETTE   1876   Oil   30⅞" x 44⅝"   Collection of John Hay Whitney, New York

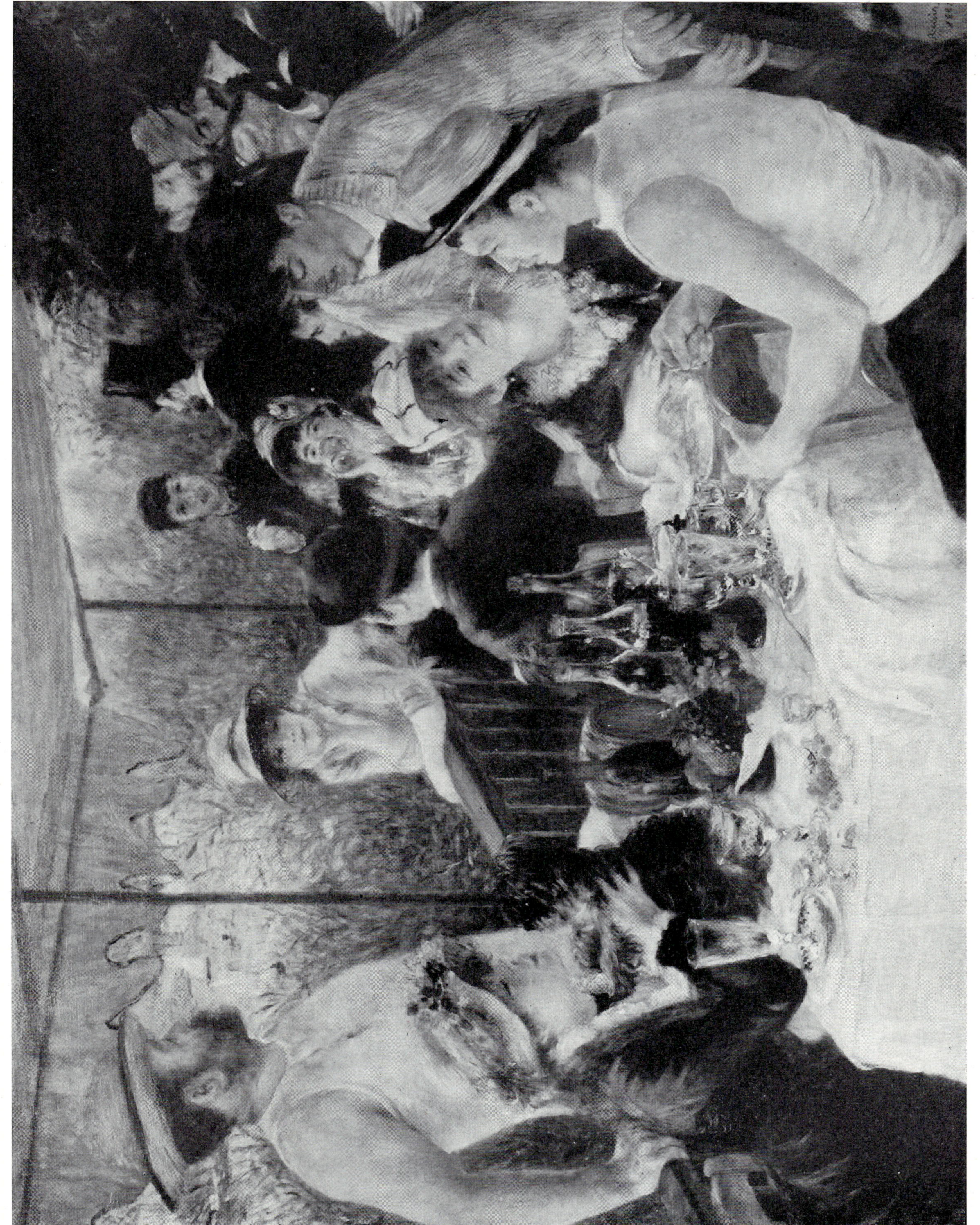

BOATING PARTY AT LUNCHEON   1881   Oil   51" x 68"
Collection of The Phillips Memorial Gallery, Washington, D. C.

MADEMOISELLE SICOT 1865 Oil 48¾" x 38¼"
National Gallery of Art, Washington, D.C., Chester Dale Collection (Loan)

FRUITS OF THE MIDI   1881   Oil   20" x 27"
The Art Institute of Chicago, Mr. and Mrs. M. A. Ryerson Collection

MADAME CHOCQUET READING   1876   Oil
25¾" x 21½"
Mrs. H. Harris Jonas, New York

43

ROSES IN A BLUE VASE

Bignou Gallery, New York

1912　Oil　20¾" x 18¼"

BATHER ARRANGING HER HAIR   Oil   35½" x 29"
The National Gallery of Art, Chester Dale Collection (Loan)

MADAME CAILLEBOTTE   1883   Oil   36¼" x 28¾"
Courtesy of Mrs. Angelika W. Frink, New York

PONT NEUF, PARIS   1872   Oil   29¼" x 36½"
Courtesy of Mr. Marshall Field, New York

FLOWERS IN A VASE Oil 31½" x 24¾"
Courtesy of Mrs. Alan Cunningham, New York